T0012094

She Plays Lacrosse

By Trudy Becker

level
2
little blue
readers

www.littlebluehousebooks.com

Little Blue House is distributed by North Star Editions:
sales@northstareditions.com | 888-417-0195

Produced for Little Blue House by Red Line Editorial.

Photographs ©: Shutterstock Images, cover, 11 (bottom), 19, 21; iStockphoto, 4, 7, 9, 11 (top), 12, 15, 16, 23 (top), 24 (top left), 24 (top right), 24 (bottom left), 24 (bottom right); Keith JJ/Pixabay, 23 (bottom)

Library of Congress Control Number: 2022910477

ISBN
978-1-64619-709-5 (hardcover)
978-1-64619-741-5 (paperback)
978-1-64619-801-6 (ebook pdf)
978-1-64619-773-6 (hosted ebook)

Printed in the United States of America
Mankato, MN
012023

About the Author

Trudy Becker lives in Minneapolis, Minnesota. She likes exploring new places and loves anything involving books.

Table of Contents

Getting Ready **5**

On the Field **13**

In the Game **17**

Glossary **24**

Index **24**

Getting Ready

I play lacrosse.

I love game days.

I get my stick.

The stick has a net on the end.

I find my uniform.

I wear a jersey.

jersey

I put on my goggles.

They keep my eyes safe.

I put on my cleats too.

They help me run fast.

I am ready to play.

goggles

cleats

field

teammate

On the Field

Games happen on the field.

I warm up with

my teammates.

I find my spot on the field.

I am excited to play.

In the Game

When games start,

I run downfield.

The ball flies in the air.
I reach out my stick and
catch it.

I twist the stick in my
hands to keep the
ball safe.
Other players can't get it.

I shoot the ball.

It flies into the goal.

I score!

I love lacrosse.

goal

Glossary

goal

jersey

goggles

stick

Index

C
cleats, 10

G
goal, 22

J
jersey, 8

S
stick, 6, 18, 20